SMILE!

ALL ABOUT TEETH

BEN HUBBARD

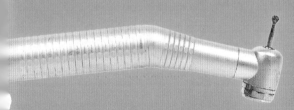

raintree

a Capstone company — publishers for children

Raintree is an imprint of Capstone Global Library Limited, a company incorporated in England and Wales having its registered office at 264 Banbury Road, Oxford, OX2 7DY – Registered company number: 6695582

www.raintree.co.uk
myorders@raintree.co.uk

Text © Capstone Global Library Limited 2019
The moral rights of the proprietor have been asserted.

Edited by Helen Cox Cannons
Designed by Cynthia Della-Rovere
Picture research by Tracy Cummins
Production by Kathy McColley
Originated by Capstone Global Library Limited
Printed and bound in India

ISBN 978 1 4747 6236 6
22 21 20 19 18
10 9 8 7 6 5 4 3 2 1

British Library Cataloguing in Publication Data
A full catalogue record for this book is available from the British Library.

Acknowledgements
We would like to thank the following for permission to reproduce photographs: Alamy: Mark Harvey, 27, Science History Images, 25 Bottom; Getty Images: AFP/RAYMOND ROIG, 7, Science Photo Library - STEVE GSCHMEISSNER, 18 Bottom; iStockphoto: kirill4mula, 19 Middle, wekeli, 11 Bottom; Shutterstock: Adalbert Dragon, 10 Left, Africa Studio, 18 Top, Air Images, 23, Anna Hoychuk, 16-17, Arve Bettum, 12, bergamont, Back Cover, Cover TR, 1 BR, botazsolti, 19 Top, bymandesigns, 13, Dionisvera 1 Top, Evgeny Atamanenko, 4-5 Background, Humannet, Cover Top Middle, Juriah Mosin, 15 Middle, Kamila Starzycka, 15 Top, konmesa, 11 Middle, La Gorda, 17 Top, Laboko, 20-21, Martin Novak, 4, michaeljung, 15 Bottom, Monkey Business Images, 5, 22, Nachaphon, Cover Bottom Middle, PavloArt Studio, 6, Peter Hermes Furian, 8-9, phochi, Design Element, Rob Byron, 21, Samuel Borges Photography, 14 Top, Satirus, 10 Right, 11 Top, Szasz-Fabian Jozsef, 19 Bottom, Tyler Olson, 25 Middle, vetkit, Cover TL, 1 BL, 24, 25 Top, Yuliia V, 28, ziggy_mars, 14 Bottom.

We would like to thank Holly Finley BDS for her invaluable help in the preparation of this book.

Every effort has been made to contact copyright holders of material reproduced in this book. Any omissions will be rectified in subsequent printings if notice is given to the publisher.

All the internet addresses (URLs) given in this book were valid at the time of going to press. However, due to the dynamic nature of the internet, some addresses may have changed, or sites may have changed or ceased to exist since publication. While the author and publisher regret any inconvenience this may cause readers, no responsibility for any such changes can be accepted by either the author or the publisher.

Some words in this book appear in bold, **like this**. You can find out what they mean by looking in the glossary.

CONTENTS

About our teeth. 4

What's in a tooth? 6

Types of teeth 8

A world of teeth 10

Two sets of teeth 12

An age of teeth 14

Feed your teeth. 16

Plaque and decay. 18

Keeping teeth clean 20

Visiting the dentist 22

Tools for teeth 24

Growing straight and strong 26

Guide to brushing your teeth 28

Quiz 29

Glossary 30

Find out more 31

Index 32

About our teeth

Teeth are very important. Without teeth, we wouldn't be able to eat. We use our teeth to bite off pieces of food and chew them. We chew by moving our jaws to grind up the food between our teeth. We also move our tongues to mix the food with **saliva**. Saliva breaks down the food for **digestion** and makes it easier to swallow. Saliva helps to clean our teeth and prevents **decay**.

Hiding teeth

When we smile or yawn, we show the world our teeth. But only the top part of each tooth can be seen. This part is called the crown. The rest of the tooth sits hidden beneath our gums. This part is called the root. The root is attached to the jawbone by **ligaments**, which stop the tooth from falling out.

CHEW IT OVER

Talking teeth

Did you know you need teeth to talk properly? This is because it is hard to make certain sounds without teeth. Try saying a word beginning with a 'V' or an 'F'. We do this by moving our bottom lip against our top teeth. Now try saying a word beginning with 'TH'. We do this by moving our tongue against our upper teeth. However, we can make words starting with 'M' or 'P' without teeth. This is why babies can say "mama" and "papa".

What's in a tooth?

Teeth are tough. They can last our whole lives if we care for them. They are made of several layers. The tough outer layer is made from enamel. Enamel is the hardest substance in the human body. It does not contain **nerves**, so is not sensitive to pain. Beneath the enamel is a layer of thick **tissue** known as dentine. Dentine contains nerve endings and is sensitive to pain. It is not as hard as enamel, but is as strong as bone.

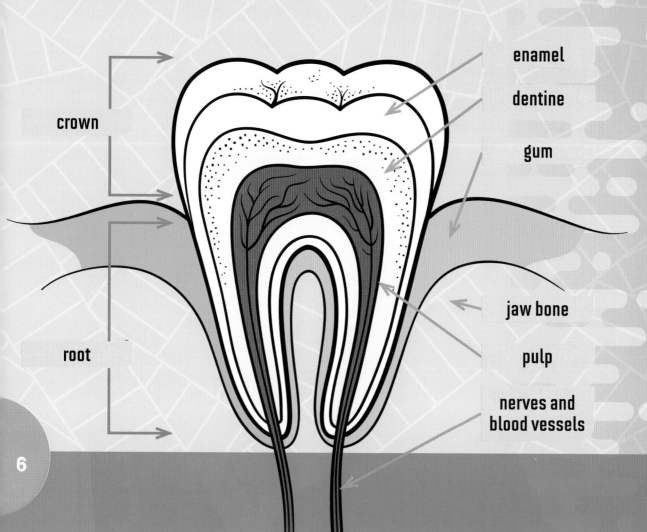

crown

root

enamel

dentine

gum

jaw bone

pulp

nerves and blood vessels

Built to last

Human teeth are tough enough to survive for hundreds of thousands of years after we die. This is because we have stopped eating food, so there is no tooth **bacteria** to cause **decay**. In 2017, two teenagers found a tooth over 560,000 years old in a cave in France. It belonged to an early kind of human.

What's inside?

At the centre of a tooth is a mass of soft tissue called the pulp. The pulp has **blood vessels** and nerves running through it. The blood vessels connect with the rest of your body and keep the tooth alive. The nerves in the pulp tell you if something is wrong. This means the pulp is very sensitive to pain. That is why the pulp is protected by the dentine and enamel outer layers.

Types of teeth

Human adults have four different types of teeth. Each one has a special shape to help us bite, crush and chew our food. This means we can eat a wide variety of foods, from tough meat to crunchy vegetables and soft fruit. So what are the four different types of teeth and where are they in our mouths?

Premolars

Behind each canine tooth are two premolars. These have a wide crown with a small cutting edge on one side. This makes them perfect for both biting and grinding up food. Children do not have premolars until they reach around 10 to 12 years old. This is when their premolars grow in with the rest of their permanent teeth (see pages 12–13).

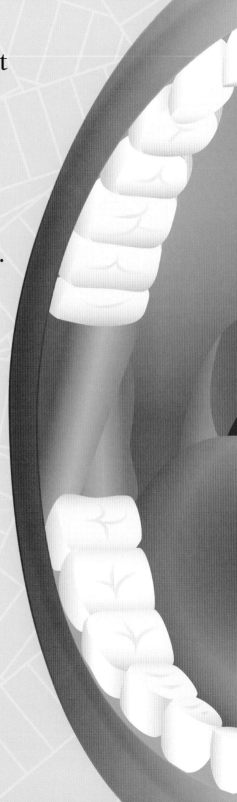

Incisors

Incisors are the teeth at the front of our mouths. Each incisor has a sharp, straight edge. We use our incisors for biting into food and cutting off chunks.

incisor

canine

premolar

molar

Canines

Canines are the teeth on either side of our incisors. They have a slightly curved, pointed edge. They are like fangs! We use our canines to stab into food and tear off small pieces.

molar

premolar

canine

incisor

Molars

At the very back of the mouth are the molars. The molars have wide, flat crowns. They are used only for crushing and grinding up food. When you close your mouth, your top and bottom molars fit together. To grind them together, we move our jaws from side to side.

A world of teeth

Humans are not the only animals with teeth. Humans are **mammals**, and most mammals have teeth. Mammals include carnivores, herbivores and omnivores. A carnivore is an animal that eats meat. A herbivore is an animal that eats plants. Omnivores eat both meat and plants. Each type has specially adapted teeth to suit the food that they eat.

Carnivores

Lions, tigers and jaguars are all carnivores. They hunt large prey such as deer, antelope and pigs. They use their long, sharp canines to kill these animals and tear off chunks of meat. Their molars also have sharp edges to slice off smaller pieces.

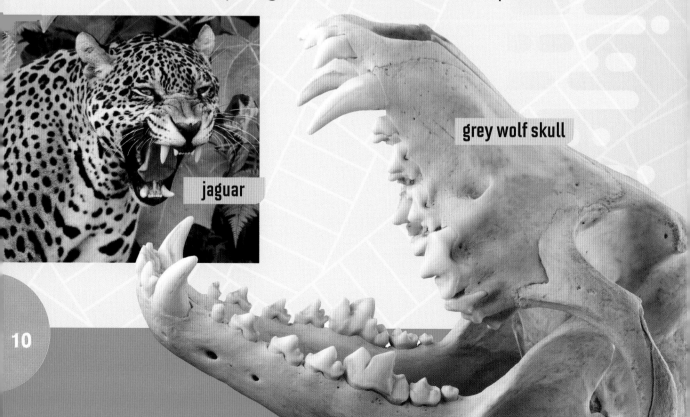

jaguar

grey wolf skull

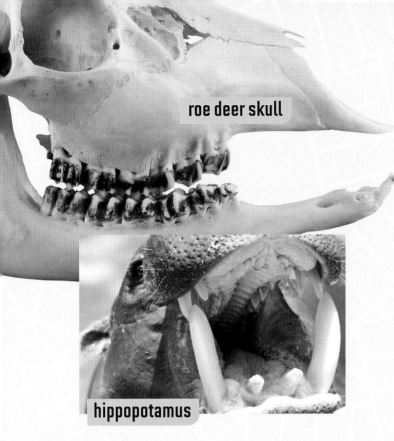

roe deer skull

hippopotamus

Herbivores

Hippopotamuses, tapirs and deer are all herbivores. They use their front incisors to bite pieces from plants. They then use their flat back molars to grind up the food. Sometimes herbivores have canine teeth, but they use them mainly for defence.

Omnivores

Humans, rats and badgers are omnivores. They eat both plants and animals. To do this, omnivores have well-adapted incisors, canines and molars to bite, crush and chew the different foods.

BITE-SIZED

Chewing like a chimp

Chimpanzees have similar teeth to people. When chimpanzees are young they have 20 teeth, just like human children. When they get older, chimpanzees grow 32 teeth, just like human adults. Their teeth are also arranged the same way as a human's. However, chimpanzees have much longer canine teeth.

11

Two sets of teeth

Humans grow two sets of teeth during their lifetimes. The first set is known as the primary, or milk teeth. As we get older, these teeth are replaced by a new set called the secondary, or permanent teeth. This happens because, as we grow, our jaws grow too. This creates more space in our mouths for our adult teeth. We have 20 milk teeth when we are young and up to 32 permanent teeth as adults.

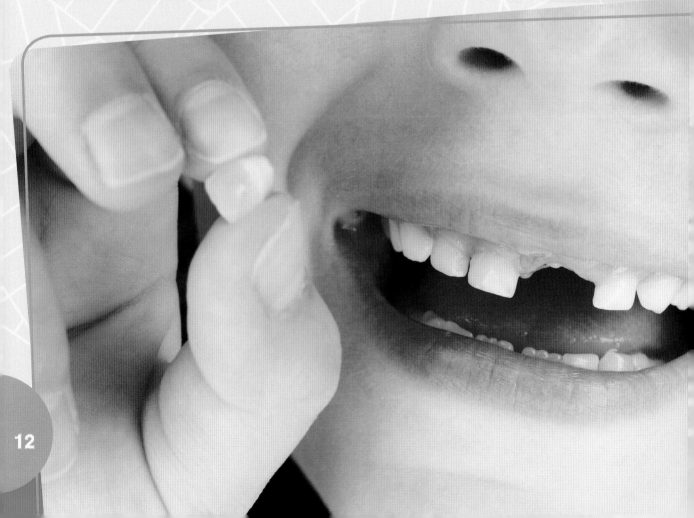

CHEW IT OVER

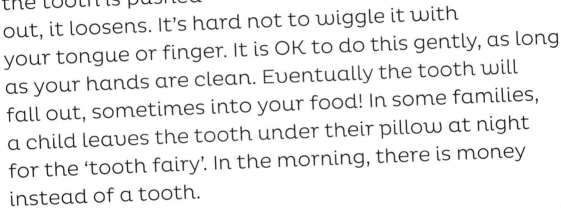

Losing a tooth

Losing a milk tooth can feel weird. As the tooth is pushed out, it loosens. It's hard not to wiggle it with your tongue or finger. It is OK to do this gently, as long as your hands are clean. Eventually the tooth will fall out, sometimes into your food! In some families, a child leaves the tooth under their pillow at night for the 'tooth fairy'. In the morning, there is money instead of a tooth.

A wiggly tooth

Milk teeth save space for the permanent teeth that grow underneath them. As a permanent tooth grows, it presses on the root of the milk tooth until it dissolves (called resorption). It then pushes the milk tooth out of the way. This is called **shedding** (also called exfoliation). Soon afterwards, the secondary tooth grows through the gum. This is called **erupting**. The x-ray image above shows a mouth with the milk teeth as well as permanent teeth waiting to come through.

An age of teeth

When babies are born, they look like they have no teeth at all. But there are teeth growing beneath the surface of their gums. As they get older, they grow their milk teeth, then lose them and grow their permanent teeth. This timeline shows at what ages these changes happen.

At birth

The crowns of the front milk teeth are nearly fully formed beneath the gums. There are 20 milk teeth altogether.

6–12 months

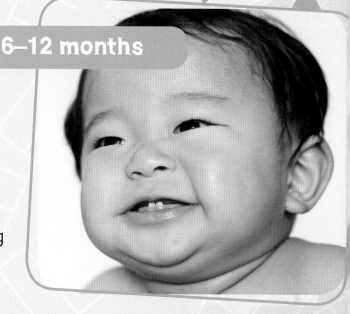

The milk teeth begin to **erupt** through the gums. The first to appear are the incisors, first molars and canines. This is called "teething". The baby's gums become sore and red during this time.

The last molars grow through the gums. All 20 milk teeth have now erupted.

6–14 years

The milk teeth begin to fall out, one at a time. Often, first the two bottom incisors and then the top incisors fall out. As the milk teeth are **shed**, new permanent teeth grow in their place. These are larger than the milk teeth and there are 28 instead of 20.

17–24 years

The final four molars grow into place. These are called wisdom teeth. Sometimes there isn't room for the wisdom teeth to erupt and they stay under the gum. Some people don't have wisdom teeth. Others have extra wisdom teeth, but this is rare.

Feed your teeth

The food that you eat has a big impact on the health of your teeth. Some foods make your teeth strong, while others attack your teeth and cause **decay**. Eating three main meals and not snacking also keeps teeth strong. This is because more **saliva** is released during a main meal. Saliva reduces tooth decay by removing harmful **acids** and cleaning **bacteria** from the teeth.

Dairy foods

Dairy foods, such as milk, cheese and yoghurt, contain a **mineral** called calcium that strengthens your teeth and your bones. Calcium can also be found in sardines, kale and watercress.

Fruit, vegetables and nuts

Nuts and vegetables are good for teeth because they increase saliva flow. Crunching carrots, celery and apples can also help clean bacteria from your teeth.

However, many citrus fruits such as oranges have high levels of acid, which can harm your teeth. Orange juice should be drunk through a straw so it spends less time on your teeth.

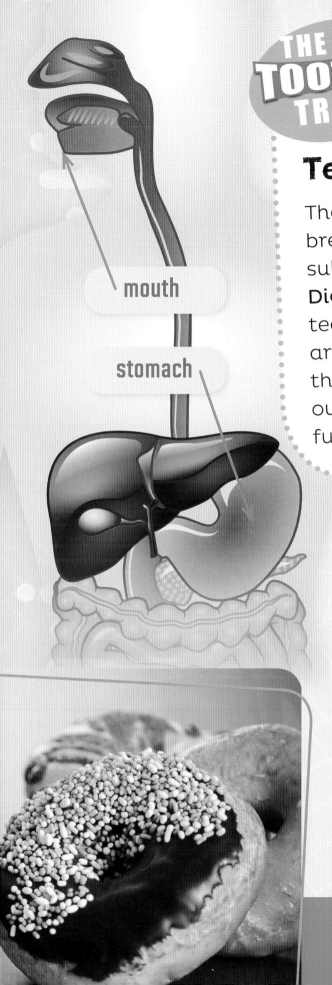

mouth

stomach

Teeth and digestion

The human digestive system breaks down food into substances our body can use. **Digestion** starts with the teeth. Chewing a mouthful around 30 times breaks down the food properly. This helps our stomachs digest the food further after it is swallowed.

Sugar

Sugary foods are very harmful to teeth. This is because sugar mixes with the bacteria on your teeth to create acid. Acid causes tooth decay. Dried fruit also does this.

Eggs, meat and fish

Eggs, meat and fish all contain a mineral called **phosphorus**, which helps keep teeth strong and healthy.

17

Plaque and decay

When adults talk about caring for teeth, they often mention the word 'plaque'. But what is it? Plaque is a sticky yellow coating that forms on our teeth and contains **bacteria**. There are around 600 types of bacteria living in our mouths. The bacteria then combine with certain foods to cause tooth **decay**. Here's how it happens.

Stage 1
When we eat a sugary and **starchy** food, it sticks onto any plaque that is coating our teeth. The food feeds the bacteria in the plaque.

Stage 2
Within seconds, the feeding bacteria begin to **multiply** and produce **harmful acids**.

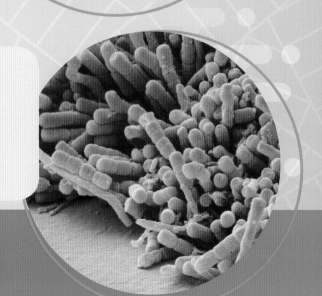

Stage 3

The acids first begin to attack the enamel layer protecting our teeth. They do this by dissolving the enamel and dentine's calcium and other **minerals**.

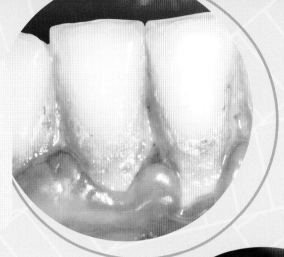

Stage 4

Over time, the acids may eat through the enamel and dentine. This causes a hole called a **cavity** to form in the tooth. The cavity will keep growing until treated by a dentist. Cavities can cause toothache and bad breath.

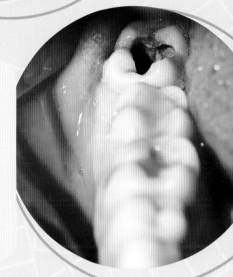

BITE-SIZED

Fill the cavity

Dentists treat cavities in your teeth by removing decayed **tissue** from around the hole. They then fill the hole with an **artificial** substance called a filling. Fillings are often made from amalgam, which is a mixture of metals. Others are made of composite, a material made from resin and powdered glass. Composite fillings are tooth-coloured so they look quite natural.

Keeping teeth clean

The best way to rid our teeth of plaque and harmful **bacteria** is to brush and floss them regularly. This helps to prevent tooth **decay** and gum disease. It is important to keep your gums healthy, as they keep your teeth attached to your jawbone.

Brushes and paste

It is best to brush your teeth with fluoride toothpaste, at least once during the day, using a regular or electric toothbrush. Brushing should also be the last thing you do before bed. This means the **fluoride** toothpaste is left on your teeth for longer. Fluoride is an important chemical that helps prevent slow tooth decay. It is sometimes added to the water supply to keep people's teeth healthy.

Feel the floss

Using dental floss or flossing sticks helps clear away food that has stuck between our teeth. It also reduces the risk of gum disease by removing plaque from around the gum line.

To use dental floss, cut off around 40 centimetres (16 inches) and wind the ends around the middle finger from each hand. Now gently slide the floss down between two teeth to the gum line and move it up and down six times. Repeat with your other teeth.

CHEW IT OVER

Disclose and dye

Disclosing tablets are made of a special **dye** that sticks to plaque. This helps to show people where they need to brush their teeth more carefully. The dye works by staining plaque with a colour, such as pink or blue. Disclosing tablets can be fun, interesting and helpful to use.

Visiting the dentist

Visiting a dentist regularly for a check-up is the best way of keeping your teeth in tip-top condition. Dentists care for your teeth and gums and make sure they are developing properly. What happens when you visit the dentist?

Examining your teeth

In the dentist's room you will lie on a big, **reclining** chair under a bright light. The dentist then examines your teeth and gums. Next to the chair is a small basin for rinsing your mouth afterwards. Sometimes the dentist takes an **X-ray** of your mouth. This is to check that your teeth are healthy and spot any **cavities**.

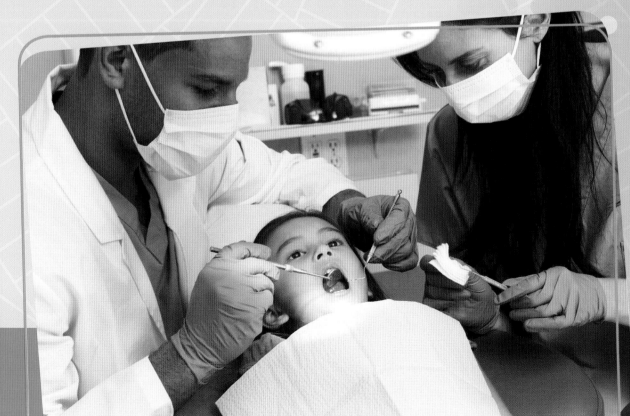

Making a diagnosis

After examining your mouth, the dentist will tell you if you need any work done. Sometimes there is a cavity in a tooth that needs a filling. There might be some stubborn plaque that needs scraping off. These are very easy things to do, so there's no need to worry.

Pink water and gritty paste

Your visit to the dentist can sometimes end with having your teeth cleaned. The dentist may recommend you see a **dental hygienist** to clean your teeth. To do this, the dentist or hygienist uses a powerful electric toothbrush with a round, spinning tip. There is special toothpaste, which can taste a little **gritty**. Afterwards, you rinse your mouth with water from a plastic cup and spit into the basin next to you. The water at the dentist is often pink!

Tools for teeth

Only 200 years ago, **blacksmiths** often did the work of dentists. If somebody's tooth was sore, the blacksmith simply pulled it out with pliers! Today, things are a lot better. Modern dentists are well trained and have the best tools to treat our teeth. These are the common ones you will see your dentist using.

Mouth mirror

This small mirror has a long handle to reach into the back of your mouth. The mirror is fitted at an angle so the dentist has a good view.

Probes and scalers

These tools have long handles and sharp points. Probes are used to feel a tooth to see if it has any **decay**. A scaler is used to scrape off plaque from teeth.

Dental drill

This small, high-speed drill removes decay from around a tooth **cavity**. This has to happen before a filling is fitted. The tooth can be numbed with special medicine so you don't feel anything.

X-ray machine

There are several types of **X-ray** machines that take images of your teeth and mouth. Some are like cameras that come up to your mouth. Others are tall machines that **revolve** around your head.

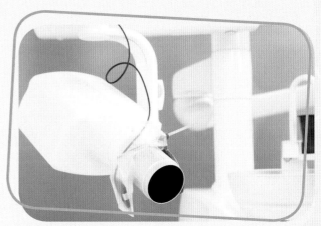

CHEW IT OVER

Your unique teeth

Did you know your teeth are **unique**? The shape of your teeth and the bite mark they leave belong only to you. In this way, they are like fingerprints.

Growing straight and strong

Sometimes when permanent teeth grow they can be crooked. This can make it hard to bite or eat comfortably. It can also make people feel **self-conscious** when they smile. Crooked teeth can be fixed by a special dentist called an **orthodontist**. Sometimes, an orthodontist may recommend getting braces fitted to straighten the teeth.

Fixed braces

Having braces fitted is common: millions of people are wearing them at this moment. There are several different types of braces. The most common are fixed braces. These have small, metal brackets that fit to each tooth so a wire can connect them. The wire puts pressure on the teeth over time to straighten them. Sometimes springs and rubber bands are also used. It can take up to two years for the teeth to straighten into the correct position. The ideal age to get braces is around 12 or 13, but it depends on the person – and the teeth!

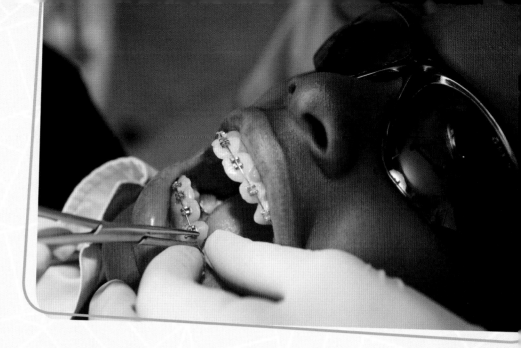

Removable braces

Removable braces can be used to correct crookedness, usually on the top row of teeth. These braces are made of plastic plates that fit into the roof of the mouth. Metal clips attached to the plates then fit over the teeth. Removable braces are worn most of the time. However, they are taken out for brushing the teeth.

BITE-SIZED

Dentures

Dentures are removable, false teeth usually made of a plastic material. They fit over a person's gums to replace missing teeth. Often older people who have lost some or all of their teeth use dentures. They take the dentures out at night to sleep.

Guide to brushing your teeth

Brushing your teeth is the best way to keep them healthy. Brushing for around two minutes during the day and before you go to bed at night is best, but you can brush at other times too. This guide will show you how best to brush.

STEP 1

Squeeze a pea-sized amount of toothpaste onto your brush.

STEP 2

Place the toothbrush against one of your front teeth and its gum. Move the toothbrush in small circles.

STEP 3

Brush the front of each of your teeth from the front of your mouth to the back, on both the top and bottom rows.

STEP 4

Now brush the biting edges of each of your teeth.

STEP 5

To clean the insides of your teeth, tilt your toothbrush and brush in small circles, as above.

STEP 6

It is best not to rinse your mouth straight after brushing. This is because rinsing will wash away the **fluoride** that is helpful for your teeth.

Quiz

Do you feel like you know all about teeth now?
Test your knowledge with this quick quiz.

1. What is the yellow coating found on teeth?

   A. Plaque
   B. Cheese
   C. Mouth dust

2. Which part of the tooth is the hardest?

   A. Dentine
   B. Enamel
   C. Pulp

3. Which is the part of a tooth you can see?

   A. Nerve
   B. Root
   C. Crown

4. Which animal has teeth the most like ours?

   A. Chimpanzee
   B. Lion
   C. Deer

5. Which food is bad for teeth?

   A. Nuts
   B. Vegetables
   C. Dried fruit

6. How many milk teeth do children have?

   A. 20
   B. 26
   C. 32

7. What are your permanent teeth sometimes called?

   A. Secondary teeth
   B. Milk teeth
   C. Primary teeth

8. When should you take out removable braces?

   A. Whenever you like
   B. When you watch TV
   C. To brush your teeth

9. How many times should we chew our food?

   A. Five times only
   B. Around 30 times
   C. Between 12 and 16 times

10. What does the dentist use a scaler for?

    A. To measure teeth
    B. To remove fish scales
    C. To remove plaque

To find out the answers to the quiz, go to page 32.

Glossary

acid liquid that can burn holes in solid things, such as teeth

artificial made by humans rather than from something natural

bacteria tiny living things that often cause disease

blacksmith person who forges metal with a hammer and anvil

blood vessel small tube that carries blood through the body

cavity hole in a tooth

decay rot

dental hygienist expert who specializes in cleaning teeth and looking after gums

digestion process of breaking down food into substances that can be used by the body

dye substance that changes the colour of something

erupt break through to suddenly appear

fluoride mineral that can help prevent cavities

gritty containing small pieces rather than smooth

ligament band of tissue that connects parts of the body, such as bone joints

mammal animal that feeds milk to its young, such as humans

mineral substance needed by the body for good health

multiply increase greatly in number

nerve tiny strand in the body that carries messages to and from the brain

orthodontist dentist who has been trained to correct crooked teeth

phosphorus mineral found in every cell of the body but mostly in the bones and teeth

reclining piece of furniture that tips back so someone can lie on it

revolve go around and around something

saliva watery liquid in the mouth used for swallowing and chewing

self-conscious feeling very aware of yourself in front of others

shed drop away

starch substance found in food such as potatoes and bread

tissue living material that animals and plants are made of

unique something that is particular to just you

X-ray photograph made by powerful rays called X-rays, which can show parts inside the body, such as bones and teeth

Find out more

Books

All About Teeth (Engage Literacy Turquoise), Jessica Holden (Raintree, 2013)

Looking After Your Teeth (Take Care of Yourself!), Sian Smith (Raintree, 2013)

Should Billy Brush His Teeth? (What Would You Do?), Rebecca Rissman (Raintree, 2013)

Wibbly Wobbly Tooth (Engage Literacy Turquoise), Jay Dale (Raintree, 2013)

Websites

bspd.co.uk
The British Society for Paediatric Dentistry website has helpful information for children and parents about children's teeth.

www.bbc.co.uk/bitesize/ks2/science/living_things/teeth_eating/read/1/
This BBC website has lots of easy-to-understand information for children about teeth and tooth care.

www.dentalbuddy.org
The Oral Health Foundation has a helpful "All About Teeth" information sheet for children and a programme about brushing teeth called "Brush Time".

Place to visit

The British Dental Museum
64 Wimpole Street
London W1G 8YS

This museum has thousands of items about the history of dentistry in the United Kingdom. It is open on Tuesdays and Thursday between 1 p.m. and 4 p.m.
bda.org/museum

Index

acids 16, 17, 18, 19

babies 5, 14
bacteria 7, 16, 17, 18, 20
bad breath 19
blood vessels 7
braces 26–27
brushing your teeth 20, 28

calcium 16, 19
canines 9, 10, 11, 14
carnivores 10
cavities 19, 22, 23, 25
chewing 4, 8, 13, 17
chimpanzees 11
crooked teeth 26–27
crowns 5, 8, 9, 14

decay 4, 7, 16, 17, 18–19, 20, 24, 25
dental drills 25
dental hygienists 23
dentine 6, 7, 19
dentists 22–23, 24–25, 26
dentures 27
digestion 4, 17
disclosing tablets 21

enamel 6, 7, 19
erupting 13, 14, 15

fillings 19, 25
flossing 21
fluoride 20, 28
food 4, 8, 9, 10, 11, 13, 16–17, 21

gum disease 20, 21
gums 5, 14, 20

herbivores 10, 11

incisors 9, 11, 14, 15

ligaments 5

mammals 10–11
milk (primary) teeth 12, 13, 14–15
minerals 16, 17, 19
molars 9, 10, 11, 14, 15
mouth mirrors 24

nerves 6, 7

omnivores 10, 11
orthodontists 26

pain 6, 7
permanent (secondary) teeth 8, 12, 13, 14, 15, 26
phosphorus 17
plaque 18, 20, 21, 23, 24
premolars 8
probes and scalers 24
pulp 7

roots 5, 13

saliva 4, 16
shedding 13, 15
sugary foods 17, 18

talking 5
teething 14

wisdom teeth 15

X-rays 22, 25